A HISTORY OF
AUSTRALIA
IN 101 OBJECTS

DAME EDNA'S
EDNAPÆDIA

A HISTORY OF
AUSTRALIA
IN 101 OBJECTS

as dictated in person to

Barry Humphries and Ken Thomson

HEAD
of ZEUS

Contents

Introduction · I

a

Aeroplane Jelly · 6
Alexander Technique · 7
Anzac · 9
Australian States · 10
Automatic Record Changer · 13

b

Backpackers · 14
Barbecue · 18
The Bee Gees · 20
Bex · 21
Big Things · 22
Billabong · 24
Black Box · 25
Black Swan · 27
Blowfly · 28
Bogans · 29
Boomerang · 30
Box Jellyfish · 33

c

Clapperboard · 37
Coogi · 38
Corroboree · 39
Crocodile · 40
Cyclone Tracy · 41

d

Didgeridoo · 44
Dingo · 47
Dog on the Tucker Box · 48
Driza-Bone · 51
Drongo · 52
Dual-flush Toilet · 53
Dunny · 55

e

Emu · 58
Escape Slide (Inflatable) · 59
Esky · 60
Etiquette (Down-Under Style) · 62

f

Fairy Penguin · 66
Foster's Lager · 67
Frilled-neck Lizard · 69

g

Galah · 72
Gladiolus · 73
Great Barrier Reef · 76
Germaine Greer · 77
Gum Tree · 78

h

Hats · 82
Hills Hoist · 86
Hoons · 89
Humidicrib · 90
Barry Humphries · 91

k

Kangaroo · 94
Kangaroo Cranes · 97
Ned Kelly · 98
Kiwi Shoe Polish · 99

Koalas · 100
Kookaburra · 103

l

Lamington · 107
Latex Gloves · 108
Lollies · 110

m

St Mary MacKillop · 114
Mallee Root · 116
Meat Pie · 117
Dame Nellie Melba · 121
Melbourne Cup · 122
Rupert Murdoch · 126

n

Neighbours · 127
New Australians · 129
Notebook · 132

o

'O' Words · 133
Ocker · 137

p

Pacemaker · 138
Pavlova · 138
Permanent Crease · 140
Phar Lap · 141
Plastic (Polymer) Bank Notes · 142
Plastic Spectacle Lenses · 145
Platypus · 146
Polly Waffle · 147
Possums · 149

r

Refrigeration · 154
ResMed · 156
Royal Flying Doctor Service · 157

s

Shark · 160
Southern Cross · 161
Speedos · 162
Spray-on Skin · 164
Joan Sutherland · 165
Swagman · 166
Sydney Funnel-web Spider · 168
Sydney Gay Pride · 170

Sydney Harbour Bridge · 172
Sydney Opera House · 173

t

Thong · 178
The Three Sisters · 179
The Twelve Apostles · 181

u

Ugg Boots · 184
Uluru · 186
Ute · 187

v

Vegemite · 190

w

Wattle · 194
Patrick White · 195
Wine Casks · 197
Woop Woop · 198
Wowsers · 199

z

Zinc Cream · 203

'You will be amazed at what my sunburnt country has contributed to civilization'

Introduction

Why, you may well ask, am I taking time off from my fabulous career to pen this book? Well, I accept I have always been a bit of an enigma, not unlike Leonardo's Gioconda – that spooky picture of a smirking Italian woman. People have been trying to get to the bottom of both of us for as long as I can remember, to plumb our depths and find out what makes us tick.

Is it nature or nurture? All I can say is that, in my case, Dame Nature must have been in a pretty good mood when she fashioned me. As for nurture – forget it! My dear mother was committed to a twilight home when I was knee-high to a grasshopper, so she cannot claim any brownie points for the Force of Nature that I have become. Like most Australian fathers, my dad was a non-starter in the cultural department, so he deserves no credit either.

I know that some carping critics and know-alls will say that Australia has moved on from the days of my childhood and motherhood, and is now the most world-class, ultra-sophisticated little country on the planet. But all I can say to these carpers is what I've always said: 'Call me old-fashioned.' By the way, possums, I myself am an Australian, and for some

'It has been pointed out that this is not a completely original idea'

people I have been the very first Australian they have come across. What a marvellous shock that must have been for them; and what an honour for me to know I personify our Broad, Brown Land.

So the book you hold so greedily in your hand is my effort to tell Australia like it is, the country that moulded – i.e. nurtured – me. A big ask, I know, but I've sifted through thousands of items for possible inclusion. From our dainty gumnuts and towering Uluru to our world-class sharks and Opera House, marauding possums and poets, taking in game-changing inventions such as the dual-flush toilet and zinc cream, you will be amazed at what my sunburnt country has contributed to modern civilization. In fact, I can say, with all modesty and without fear of successful contradiction, that almost everything worth mentioning has been invented by my countrymen – or womenfolk.

It has been pointed out by some smart alecks that this compendium of a hundred-odd things is not a totally original idea. I accept that and admit that my late bridesmaid, Mrs Madge Allsop, before she was gathered, was halfway through compiling a book entitled *A History of New Zealand in 15 Objects*.

Dame Edna Everage
Cap Ferrat and Moonee Ponds

Aeroplane Jelly

This is a dessert item and the inspiration for a quaint Australian folk song from 1938, and well-known by housewives of the 1940s since it was played more than a hundred times a week on Australian radio:

I've got a song that won't take very long,
Quite a good sort of note if I strike it. . .
It is something we eat, and I think it's quite sweet,
And I know you are going to like it.

I like Aeroplane Jelly
Aeroplane Jelly for me.

I like it for dinner, I like it for tea,
A little each day is a good recipe.
The quality's high as the name will imply,
And it's made from pure fruits, one more good
    reason why

I like Aeroplane Jelly
Aeroplane Jelly for me.

Words and music by Albert Francis Lenertz (1891–1943)

'I think I can claim I invented "poise" as we know it'

Alexander Technique

Fortunate people who have seen my wonderful stage show all comment on my posture. I think I can claim that I invented 'poise' as we know it, certainly in the Southern Hemisphere, my preferred stamping ground. If you haven't been blessed with bone structure such as mine, not to mention my charisma, you can always develop poise. I acquired mine, spookily enough, on my honeymoon in Tasmania. Unfortunately, my husband, the late Lord Norm Everage of Moonee Ponds, was not there at the time, having had one of his early urological incidents. But I went anyway, as a passage had been booked on the *Spirit of Tasmania* and we had reserved the honeymoon cabin, which had a large porthole – useful in the almost guaranteed event of a tummy upset during the rough crossing through the Bass Strait.

On the trip I hooked up with a senior citizen called F. M. Alexander, who was born in Tasmania and who passed on his technique to me, demonstrating some postural exercises which have kept me erect, serene and generally fit ever since. Many

Alexander Technique drills involve lying on the floor with a book under your head. Experienced travellers know that this can be hazardous, particularly in a cabin or a hotel suite, when you're lying there with your head on a Gideon bible and a maid comes in with a trolley to refresh the minibar and stumbles over you, causing a dozen miniatures of vodka, gin, whisky, advocaat and Bailey's Irish Cream to crash to the floor.

'If you haven't been blessed with bone structure such as mine, not to mention my charisma, you can always develop poise'

Anzac

The Australian and New Zealand Army Corps, as the name suggests, is an Australian outfit, and you'd be hard-pressed to find an Eskimo or Tunisian Anzac. There is one day in the year, 25 April, which is still sacred for Australians, as that is when we celebrate our wartime sacrifices. When I was a bubba, knee-high to a grasshopper, I asked my wonderful mother why all those men were marching or shuffling. She said: 'It's for the fallen, Edna. We are remembering the fallen.' 'But why couldn't they get up again?' I asked her, with childish innocence. 'One of these days, Edna, your father will give you a book.' This was the stock answer to all my questions – especially my habitual 'How are babies made?' query. I never did receive that book, and only after three kiddies did I begin to have an inkling about this overrated topic.

Australian States
(and a couple of Territories)

Australia is not just one continent but a conglomerate of parts, each with its own distinctive culture, dialect and populace. We have affectionate, playful nomenclature that embraces all of these diverse communities. Though partly on the whimsical side, hopefully it describes their special skills and attributes.

The inhabitants of the Northern Territory are, for example, imaginatively called 'Top-Enders' since, in most atlases, the Northern Territory occupies the upper part of Australia.

Moving clockwise around our island continent, Queenslanders are delighted to be referred to as 'Banana-Benders' or 'Cane Toads'. Since records began, the ubiquitous Queensland banana, with its distinctive curve, has been believed by the indigenous Australians to be the inspiration for their trusty boomerang (q.v.). However, a tribal elder known as 'NA-NA' recently dismissed this as 'paper talk'.

New South Welshmen and -women are known as 'Cockroaches' or 'Coathangers', after the popular local insect and the world's heaviest Sydney-based bridge.

Moving on down to my home state of Victoria, we are affectionately referred to as 'Mexicans' or 'Gumsuckers', since some of the original settlers (who were tourists, *not* convicts) were sometimes obliged to seek nutriment in unusual, but readily available, forms. Percy Grainger, our internationally acclaimed and award-winning world-class composer, wrote a wonderful piece called 'The Gumsucker's March', which to this day Melbourne mothers and homemakers croon to their bassineted bubbas.

Tasmania, the triangular and tuffeted appendage to Australia and Antarctica that, as often as not, is left off maps and globes, was once the world's largest apple-growing region. So it will come as no surprise that its rosy-cheeked inhabitants are known as 'Apple Eaters'. Less acceptable is the appellation 'Two Headers', an offensive reference to the progeny of many Tasmanians, who have a habit of 'keeping it in the family' thanks to either isolation, perversity or their fondness for a cuddle with their immediate loved ones.

South Australians are 'Crow Eaters' for obvious reasons. Then, crossing the desert, we arrive in Western Australia, home to its inhabitants the 'Sand Gropers', who are named after a grotesque burrowing insect that can only be found there. Mind you, I'd burrow myself if I looked anything like them!

And we must not forget our Capital Territory, whose hard-working civil servants are known as 'Roundabout-Abouters' or 'Bouters' due to their path-breaking traffic system.

'New South Welshmen and women are known as "Cockroaches" or "Coathangers", after the popular local insect and the world's heaviest Sydney based-bridge'

Automatic Record Changer

I was pretty hyperactive when I was knee-high to a grasshopper and was always wittering away about my theatrical ambitions, goals, boundaries and eventual Superstardom. This got on my mother Gladys's nerves. She was going through The Change and would grow impatient with me, perhaps understandably in hindsight. 'Change the record, Edna!' she used to snap. Imagine my surprise when, coincidentally, none other than a Tasmanian inventor, Eric Waterworth, came up with an invention in 1925 – the Salonola – which did just that, changing old shellac discs automatically! We all had stacks of these records and it was a relief to be able to listen to five of them without having to get up from the comfort of your sofa. We knew an Austrian immigrant who had all sixteen hours of Wagner's Ring Cycle on disc: he was even more exhausted by hopping up and down than he would have been by attending a 'flesh and blood' performance!

Sadly, the Salonola *per se* never reached the shops because the original company was liquidated. Undeterred, in typical

'These days the young folk have no idea what you're on about when you use expressions such as "Change the record"'

Tazzie style the Waterworths upped sticks and travelled to London, where the Symphony Gramophone and Radio Company snapped up Eric's game-changing invention – and the rest is history, possums.

These days, in a world of streaming, downloading, etc., the young folk have no idea of what you're on about when you use expressions such as 'Change the record', and when folk go on and on about something and repeating themselves, and you snap, 'Sounds like your needle's got stuck,' the kiddies roll their eyes and look at you as though you're from another planet.

Backpackers

Backpackers are Australians abroad and, let's face it, New Zealanders as well. There are so many of the latter away from home that I often wonder if there is anyone left in sleepy New Zealand. Despite their heavy encumbrances, backpackers are not necessarily going anywhere. I'm told that if you travel on the underground or subway (heaven forbid!), you could get smashed in the face by a swiftly turning backpacker who is going no further than the office. It's a look I can't stand, but I suppose it makes people feel they're still at school with a satchel slung over their shoulders. Nothing amuses me more than seeing a backpacker on his back having fallen over and struggling to get up like an overturned tortoise!

'Nothing amuses me more than seeing a backpacker on his back and struggling to get up like an overturned tortoise'

Barbecue
(or barbie)

I cannot speak about barbecues first-hand because they are usually a male event held outside in the blazing sun, accompanied by large quantities of alcohol, and ladies are generally not included unless we are required to make the salads and toss or do the washing-up afterwards. Frankly, I don't enjoy barbies, even from a distance. But rats do, and it has been conclusively proven to be the number-one attraction for these particular vermin, who can creep into backyards and gobble up the leftovers while the human barbie guests are sleeping off the booze. A wise person once said – and it was probably me – that the food served at barbecues is not the type of provender you would ever dream of serving and eating indoors in a nice home – and certainly *never* in mine!

The Bee Gees

Not to be confused with that ghastly bunch the Heebie Jeebies, the Bee Gees were a delightful group of young brothers of British origin who performed and composed most of the twentieth century's best pop music, including the soundtrack of *Saturday Night Fever*, starring my bosom buddy and god-daughter Olivia Newton-John. Bee Gees was an abbreviation of Brothers Gibb. My bridesmaid Madge adored them and had to be shooed away for making a nuisance of herself at the stage door of any venue in which they were performing. She took it rather hard but continued to worship them till the day she was gathered.

Bex

A universal analgesic, the Australian housewife's drug of choice in the 1950s and '60s. These homemakers would take it in vast quantities to alleviate the extreme stress of living in suburban Australia. In 1965, the Sydney playwright and wag John McKellar wrote a celebrated comedy revue called *A Cup of Tea, a Bex and a Good Lie Down* celebrating the use of this popular drug, in the road-testing of which my mother was a willing and notable pioneer. *A Good Lie Down* was, as often not, beside a dialysis machine.

'Homemakers would take it in vast quantities to alleviate the extreme stress of living in suburban Australia'

Big Things

My homeland of Australia is a big place, so no wonder it produces such outsize talent in every field! The roads and highways often feature very large replicas of some of our national treasures, and the bigger the better, including the Big Banana, the Big Pineapple, the Big Prawn, the Big Funnel-Web Spider, the Big Merino Sheep and the Big Cockroach. These days many of them are made of fibreglass and contain visitor centres, where postcards, oven mitts, keyrings, snowstorms and other tasteful souvenirs can be purchased by awestruck and appreciative tourists. Most are wheelchair accessible.

The Authorities of my home suburb, Moonee Ponds (which I put on the map), have approached me about erecting a Big Edna at the entrance to the neighbourhood which would contain not only the traditional souvenir shops but also pizzerias, bowling alleys, tattoo parlours and meditation centres, but I am still mulling it over. To be frank, I'm not that keen on having an observation deck on my upper lip.

'The Authorities have approached me about erecting a Big Edna'

Billabong

'Billabong' is an Aboriginal word and a popular way of describing a loop in a river that becomes isolated. It often dries up and is frequently the camping ground of the odd 'jolly swagman' (q.v.). When it holds water, it is usually stagnant and infested with mozzies. My home suburb of Moonee Ponds is situated on an ancient billabong of the Maribyrnong River. My wonderful mother's face was often likened to an aerial view of Moonee Ponds in the Jurassic period, and she always liked to say that the lines on her face were the dried-up beds of old smiles.

'It is usually stagnant and infested with mozzies'

Black Box

The black box is a contraption that records the scr*ams, pr*yers and fo*r-letter w*rds of pilots who experience turbulence or have taken a wrong turn. David Warren invented the black box (actually orange – don't ask, possums!) after his dad perished in one of Australia's pioneering air crashes in 1926. Australians didn't think much of this invention, but it was picked up by the Brits and manufactured in the US. I have one in my limo but I'm not sure I'd like all my conversations recorded and ending up on the Internet. I like to think that what's said in a limo stays in a limo. Madge – my bridesmaid – was my driver for many years, and I had to give her the rough edge of my tongue on more than one occasion. I certainly would not like that in cyberspace!

Black Swan

The black swan is native to Australia, but due to the iniquitous White Swan Policy (1901–58) I never saw one during my childhood. They are still mostly found hiding out in Western Australia and adorn the emblems of that state.

'Due to the iniquitous White Swan Policy I never saw one during my childhood'

Blowfly
(dunny budgie)

A chubby, bird-like insect popular in all Australian cities and country towns, its cheerful buzz can often be heard in massed chorus in the vicinity of faecal matter and scrumptious meals alike. The outdoor toilet was historically a popular rendezvous for the blowie, so they came to be known as 'dunny budgies'. Australian housewives and homemakers alike often find their principal household duty is to discourage blowies from alighting on freshly made meals, where, knowing no better, they generally go to the toilet. Tourist brochures rarely mention these intriguing creatures, so their mass descent on Overseas nostrils, lips, corneas, etc., is often an unwelcome surprise. The cork-trimmed hat was an ancient deterrent, but it is no longer worn and most native Australians now discourage these relentless swarms with a constant wave of the hand in front of their faces – an action that has become officially known as the Outback Salute.

Bogans

Unsavoury Australian yobbos, or persons my mother used to call 'c-o-m-m-o-n' (she always spelt it out). At first used to describe any male person from West Melbourne (Westies), it has become universal thanks to the decline of etiquette and standards of dress in public places. The bogan is a descendant of the 1950s phenomenon the 'bodgie' – an habitué of sleazy milk bars and consort of the slatternly 'widgie'. There is currently a fear that the boganization of Australia is well advanced, and in recent years the prime ministers of the Australia have exhibited the characteristics of truculence, slovenly speech and near illiteracy that was originally the preserve of the bogan community.

> NB: Bogans have no connection whatsoever with the fragrant yet garishly coloured bougainvillea, which some people have the barefaced cheek to assert is more beautiful than the gladiolus.

'Persons my mother used to call "c-o-m-m-o-n"'

Boomerang

The boomerang is a wooden instrument shaped like a boomerang. It is a missile which our wonderful indigenous people have been trying to get rid of for millennia. And without any success, since it has a nasty habit of whizzing back to the Aboriginal who has been trying to dispose of it. In its flight it can seriously maim a large grazing marsupial. I have never disclosed this before, but it is just possible that in the far distant past one of my ancestors was a member of the indigenous community – perhaps the Mooneewarra tribe. So I like to say, without risk of successful contradiction, that I have a little Aborigine in me. In my case, the Aboriginal part of me can *throw* a boomerang, but, with my Anglo-Saxon roots, it never ever comes back. It is no surprise, then, that one of my favourite pop tunes is Mr Charlie Drake's moving 'My Boomerang Won't Come Back' (google it, possums, I haven't got room for it here).

'A missile which our wonderful indigenous people have been trying to get rid of for millennia'

Box Jellyfish

Luckily, these ghastly pests never cropped up in the waters of Melbourne's Port Phillip, where our family often went for a dip, and they were a very good reason why we never wished to visit Queensland. Even today, you might not come back if you encounter one of these horrendous creatures. Most of Australia's world-class beaches have emergency facilities to treat swimmers – or remnants of swimmers – who have been molested by the transparent and sometimes minute jellyfish, which are also known as the 'suckerpunch'. Fortunately, they have yet to be found in our suburban swimming pools.

'A very good reason why we never wished to visit Queensland'

Clapperboard

This major accoutrement of the film industry was invented in Australia by a member of a legendary Australian theatrical family, the Thrings, which included a one-time friend of mine. It is used in the film-making process every time a scene is shot. No modern technique has replaced the clapperboard, whose name comes from the snapping sound it makes to signal the start of filming. I often think I would like to have one to shut people up when I am talking.

The origin of this Australian invention is disputed by jealous nations: for once New Zealand *hasn't* lodged a claim.

'The origin of this Australian invention is disputed by jealous nations: for once New Zealand hasn't lodged a claim'

Coogi

Fashionable multi-coloured sweaters originally designed in the uber-affluent Melbourne suburb of Toorak with a distinctive decorative style resembling multi-coloured viscera ingeniously entwined. The brand – originally named Cuggi, but changed to Coogi to make it sound more 'indigenous' – is now owned by an American company, and the label can now also be found in other garments and footwear. The Coogi sweater makes it possible not only to wear your heart on your sleeve, but also your liver, lungs, large intestines and organs including your spleen.

> NB: Wealthy modern-day denizens of highly-desirable Toorak may not be pleased to learn that it is suggested that the name of their suburb means 'reedy swamp' or 'duckweed' in the local Aboriginal language. It's a case, as I often say, of 'from effluence to affluence'.

Corroboree

A ceremony performed by our wonderful, world-class, ground-breaking indigenous Australians, who used to be called Aborigines. I've never actually been to a corroboree, but most tourists naturally do their best to include one in their itinerary, along with visits to the penguins (q.v.) on Phillip Island, the polyps on the Great Barrier Reef (q.v.) and to the Sydney Opera House (q.v.). More intrepid souls may visit the quokkas on Rottnest Island (Dutch: rat's nest).

Corroborees are apparently very lively events, if a bit drawn out. In the 1940s, they inspired the Australian composer John Antill to write the ballet *Corroboree*, which involved Australian ballet dancers dressing up as indigenous Australians. However, this process of maquillage is thought to be no longer politically correct, so this wonderful, internationally acclaimed ballet has been by and large dropped from the repertoire.

'Corroborees are apparently very lively events, if a bit drawn out'

Crocodile

Many of Australia's northern beaches would be incomplete without a colony of man-eating reptiles. These creatures are completely harmless, unless they run after you and give you a nip as you attempt to scramble up a nearby tree. The promotion and ensuing popularity of crocodile skin as a material for top-of-the-range accessories for us women has not endeared us to the reptilian community. In the wild, these animals are so dangerous that our indigenous folk have devised an ingenious way of testing the water before entering: they throw in a dog, or dingo (q.v.), and if it is still swimming five minutes later they sound the all-clear to their amphibious colleagues.

'These creatures are completely harmless, unless they run after you and give you a nip as you attempt to scramble up a nearby tree'

Cyclone Tracy

The city of Darwin, which Australians very rarely visit, has been the target of two serious assaults: first by the Japanese air force during the Second World War; and, later, by Cyclone Tracy. When I first went there, I took in an important exhibition containing Traciana at the Darwin library, where local families and the odd tourist could marvel at chilling dioramas and re-live the terrors of Tracy. Most popular was a reconstructed suburban living room, or 'lounge room', which graphically illustrated the ravages wrought by the cyclone. There was an overturned chair, a crooked lampshade and a wrecked twenty-one-inch Astor TV set, behind the shattered screen of which the imaginative curators affixed a photograph of the smiling face of a one-time revered television personality. There was also a rumpled carpet and broken venetian blinds. 'Mummy, that's just like our place,' a darling Aboriginal child was once overheard to exclaim during a government-sponsored visit to the facility.

Tracy struck on Christmas Eve 1974, which inspired a moving song: 'Santa Never Made It into Darwin'.

Didgeridoo

The didgeridoo, or drone pipe, is a hollowed-out branch made from the finest eucalyptus tree through which members of our superbly musical indigenous community blow to spooky effect. I personally have heard it played by a close Aboriginal friend of mine on a moonlit night in the Outback, and it was one of the most moving moments of my entire life. Music buffs have likened the didgeridoo to an ethnic bassoon. This instrument should never be judged by the performances given daily by amateur practitioners at Sydney's Circular Quay, just a stone's throw from, and within earshot of, that cauldron of musical culture, the Sydney Opera House (q.v.). These Aboriginal impersonators blow their hearts out, accompanied by deafening boombox amplification.

I hate to bring myself into these absorbing entries now and then, but it might be useful to my readers to hear that, according to a 2005 article in the *British Medical Journal*,

'The word didgeridoo is a loose English translation of the original Aboriginal "didgeridu"'

learning and practising the didgeridoo can help reduce snoring. *You can tell that to the marines!* My last husband Norm was famously noisy in bed: his snoring sometimes drowned out the noise of his prostate murmur. So, when I was sent the *BMJ* article by my fellow sufferer and bridesmaid Madge Allsop, I purchased from Amazon a top-of-the-range digital didgeridoo. It did decrease Norm's somnolent sonority, but I soon got sick and tired of being poked by his giant instrument between the sheets, so it was either it or me who had to go. And I leave you to guess which one, possums!

NB: By the way, the word 'didgeridoo' is a loose English translation of the original Aboriginal 'didgeridu'.

'This instrument should never be judged by the performances given daily by amateur practitioners at Sydney's Circular Quay'

Dingo

The dingo is an Australian wild dog and certainly not the kind you pat. It is a rather horrible yellow colour – a bit like sick or something you might find on the pavement outside one of Australia's world-class gastropubs, where some of the patrons have had tummy upsets. The publicity Australian dingoes received in 1980, when little Azaria Chamberlain disappeared from her bassinet in the Outback, inspired the famous and moving song 'The Dingo Ate My Baby'.

'It is a rather horrible yellow colour – a bit like something you might find on the pavement outside one of Australia's world-class gastropubs'

Dog on the Tucker Box

Jack O'Hagan, the singer and songwriter – Australia's Irving Berlin – wrote a jaunty song dedicated to the country town of Gundagai, where a dog loyally guarded his owner's tucker box. The lyrics ran:

I'm just a love-lorn weary coot and I've composed
*   a song,*
It's all about a girl I love and dream of all day long –
The rhythm seemed to come to me whilst milking
*   fav'rite cow –*
And as my hands went up and down I wrote this
*   song I vow.*

My Mabel waits for me underneath the bright blue sky,
Where the dog sits on the tucker box five miles from
*   Gundagai –*
I meet her every day and I know she's dinky di –
Where the dog sits on the tucker box five miles from
*   Gundagai.*

'Why even Shakespeare never wrote a poem as good as this'

Now poets in the days gone by were often much inspired
By lovely wenches that they loved and otherwise
*   admired.*
But though they wrote some lovely prose whilst in
*   a state of bliss,*
Why even Shakespeare never wrote a poem as good
*   as this.*

The tucker box was the forerunner of today's boxes which are mounted on a fence post at the gates of many Australian rural properties for the acceptance of deliveries. There is still, very close to the town of Gundagai, the effigy of a dog that inspired O'Hagan; and this is now a touristic imperative, particularly popular with Koreans, who are frequently disappointed by the unpalatable nature of this Australian icon. Some uncalled-for folk have suggested that the verb 'sat' was actually a little longer and included another letter. But let's not go there, possums.

Driza-Bone

This is an garment made of cotton, with an oil and wax finish, that, by a spooky coincidence, keeps the wearer as DRY AS A BONE. Say the name Driza-Bone very slowly, possums, and you will get what I mean. It was invented as long ago as 1898 and was an immediate godsend to our explorers, sailors and stockmen. As has been said by wiser souls than I, it also clothed the men who built the railways and highways of Australia, served in two world wars and travelled with explorers to and from the vast icy sheets of Antarctica and the snowy peaks of the Himalayas.

'By a spooky coincidence, keeps the wearer as DRY AS A BONE'

Drongo

It is significant and perhaps not altogether to our credit that we Australians have a plethora of words to describe stupid people, losers and no-hopers, or, to be frank, possums, folk who are one prawn short of a barbie or even with kangaroos loose in the top paddock. This is paradoxical given that the Australian intelligentsia is world-class. Australia is the cultural capital of the world, and many of these epithets are regional: for example, a 'droob' is a Western Australian drongo, or 'dill', although 'dags' are nationwide. Possibly the most intellectually challenged community is that of the drongo. Many people consulting this book may be unaware that they were named after a 1920s horse called Drongo, which was bred from a mare named Lillie Langtry, Oscar Wilde's preferred performer. Drongo never even won a race. . .

Dual-flush Toilet

This ground-breaking gizmo is one of Australia's proudest inventions, conserving precious water and enabling the thoughtful visitor, at the touch of a finger, to select a flow of water appropriate to his or her most recent evacuation. Imagine the hours of harmless fun, exertion and strain its inventor, Bruce Thompson, enjoyed perfecting his brainchild!

'This groundbreaking gizmo is one of Australia's proudest inventions'

Dunny

Not a word I care for, or use. Apparently, in the Olden Days 'dunny' was always on the lips of Yorkshire folk in the Mother Country. It originates from the British dialect word 'dunnekin', which was a ditch convicts brought out with them on their early trips to Australia. It became the universal Australian term for an outdoor toilet, and to this day it is used in south Sydney to describe an indoor one as well. When I was knee-high to a grasshopper I was taken into the bush for a weekend to see old Auntie Liddy, and my mother was disappointed – and rather put off – to find her facility was in a small shed in the backyard, with no sign of toilet paper and just an old phone book on a nail. The Yellow Pages used to be pink at that time, but in a dunny the colour of the toilet paper is immaterial. Also, a yucky flypaper curled from the ceiling, encrusted with struggling blowies (q.v.). It put Yours Truly off the Outback for life. Since then, the dunny has come of age, and nowadays house-proud and sophisticated Australian homemakers always fold the end of their hygienic tissue into a neat little triangle.

Emu

The emu is the tallest bird in the world, despite stubborn claims to the contrary by adherents to the Tall Ostrich Theory. Unlike the cowardly ostrich, the Australian emu never puts its head in the sand when danger approaches. It has no need to be so retiring since, incidentally, and to boot, it has the second-strongest legs in the world.

The emu feather is attached to the slouch hats worn by the diggers of the Australian Light Horse. Their diet – the birds', that is – includes beer bottles, nails and small components of Toyotas, all of which enhance their digestive capacity. 'May your chooks turn into emus and kick your dunny down!' is an often used and, to my mind, unpleasant Australian curse.

'The emu is the tallest bird in the world, despite stubborn claims to the contrary'

Escape Slide (Inflatable)

Many satisfied airline passengers have been grateful for this typically practical and thoughtful Australian aid. Stewardesses and stewards of the past and, more recently, members of the 'in-flight executive community' always enjoy assisting passengers in their egress from a temporarily disabled aircraft, urging passengers to remove high heels and winkle-pickers, strap on their lifebelts and hope for the best as they disembark, sliding precipitously into shark-infested waters.

'Many airline passengers have been grateful for this typically practical and thoughtful Australian aid'

Esky

In my day we used to have delightful picnics, usually in a bushland setting, where we managed to enjoy ourselves without the use of an Esky. Although arguably invented in America, nowadays it is an essential piece of equipment for every Australian family. Comprising a portable box that is insulated to keep the contents cold, it is very popular with sippers and folk addicted to the liquid lunch. It comes in handy on the beach, where a stash of beer and wine is kept and even some soft drinks for kiddies and seniors, and sometimes there is just enough room to slip in a sandwich or two.

The word 'Esky' is derived from Eskimo, a species alien to Australia and Antarctica. These days Eskimos prefer to be called Inuits, but the portable fridge has retained its original name.

'Very popular with sippers and folk addicted to the liquid lunch'

Etiquette
(Down-Under Style)

Australians are renowned for their politeness, and my personal niceness is legendary. So readers will be interested to hear of a case in point:

On his return from a trip Overseas, some time in the mid-1990s – he dates it as about midday on 30 June 1995 – Stan Ramsgate, the deputy manager of Brisbane's prestigious Crest Hotel, called an emergency three-line-whip meeting with his staff. Top of the agenda – the only item, in fact – was the order that, henceforward, the time-honoured Australian expression 'no worries' should not pass from their lips and should be replaced by the more genteel, acceptable, international 'not a problem, sir/madam/doctor/your honour (or whatever)'. This locution spread throughout the Australian hospitality community like bush fire, and soon the whole continent (including Perth and the whole of Tasmania) had adopted

'My personal niceness is legendary'

this comforting neologism, even when there actually *was* a problem. Since then, the expression has gone global and viral. It has also proven to be an all-purpose exculpatory locution.

> PS: I hope I'm not going over some of my readers' heads (figuratively speaking) with some of the words that spring from my lips so effortlessly. Sorry, possums, but they do.

Fairy Penguin

An imperative on a Japanese tourist's itinerary is to view the world's tiniest penguin, the fairy penguin, which inhabits Phillip Island, off the coast of my home state, Victoria, as well as other spots in Australia. These gorgeous little blue-hued creatures are bred exclusively for the tourist trade, which feeds them copious amounts of government-approved performance enhancers, thus ensuring they always put on a good show for their insatiable, mainly Oriental, audiences.

Foster's Lager

An obscure beverage brewed by Carlton and United Breweries and unknown outside Melbourne until Barry Humphries (q.v.), my erstwhile manager and alter ego, went on and on about it in a *Private Eye* comic strip in the 1960s. Concerned about its image, the brewery attempted to downplay Humphries's snide and lager-fuelled comments. But the damage had been done and Foster's lager became synonymous with beer worldwide. Finding that, thanks to Humphries, there was international demand for the product, the bewildered brewer employed Paul Hogan (an actor) to make advertisements promoting its lager in the colloquial, proletarian Australian vernacular. I am happy to tell you that Humphries himself received not a single penny from the profits he had inadvertently fostered. For the record, possums, it's not my cup of tea.

'For the record, possums, it's not my cup of tea'

Frill-necked Lizard
(chlamydosaurus kingii)

Many Japanese folk come to Australia not merely to survey the large tracts of land that they own but also to fondle and photograph their favourite reptile, the insectivorous frill-necked lizard. They seem to find it funny to disturb the creature, thus provoking a dramatic and over-the-top deimatic display (from the lizard, not the tourist). This is also observed when the lizards are trying for a family. One of their main predators – apart from camera-toting tourists – is the dreaded marsupial, the quoll.

'One of their main predators – apart from camera-toting tourists – is the dreaded marsupial, the quoll'

Galah

A popular, colourful Australian parrot fitted out in retro kitsch 1950s pink and grey livery, the galah, unlike other parrots, lacks the power of speech and is therefore assumed to be of low intellect, hence the popular phrase, 'You silly/stupid/great galah!' Our world-class, cutting-edge indigenous community include the meat of the galah in many of their scrumptious concoctions. It goes without saying the parrot must be deceased before ingestion.

'It goes without saying the parrot must be deceased before ingestion'

Gladiolus

It would be impertinent and an insult to my native land to omit the gladiolus, or gladdie, from this tome. When the English poet Rossetti went on about 'lilies of the field', many scholars determined that the original biblical Aramaic should have been translated as 'gladdies of the field'. Although, strictly speaking, the gladiolus is not a native Australian flower, it is identified the world over with the land of my birth – and with Yours Truly in particular. In the 1950s, when the popularity of the gladdie was at an all-time low and there were real fears among the horticultural community of its possible extinction, I devoted an entire show to this beautiful, aggressive flower. Florists and gladdie-watchers are aware, of course, that the gladiolus is, in horticultural terms, a bisexual corm, but I personally have never held that against it (though if there are children or senior citizens around and a vase of gladdies, as a rule I cover the flowers up at night in case they get up to something uncalled for).

History does not record how Australia first got its gladdies, but its favourite form of propagation is via the corm, which may have floated over to Australia from Africa in what is technically known as the Olden Days. There are certainly

early Aboriginal rock paintings of what are thought to be gladdies in the hands of warriors and their dusky concubines. Man discovered the versatility and multitasking ability of the gladiolus, or 'sword lily', in the Jurassic period. The dried corm and rhizome, ground to a fine powder, became a popular aphrodisiac, and there was no stopping the production of this popular product, which has been rediscovered by hippies in their Outback habitats, where gladdies are grown in profusion. My favourite is the flesh-pink variety, which I began to hurl at my gorgeous audiences in the dozens in the swinging 1960s. I continue the custom today, pelting my grateful public with thousands of these expensive blooms.

'It would be impertinent and an insult to my native land to omit the gladiolus, or gladdie, from this tome'

Great Barrier Reef

No book about Australia would be complete without reference to the Great Barrier Reef. Australian polyps are proud of their spectacular achievement (polyp power), and if it were not for this construction, our tourist income would be nil. Visitors are often surprised that the reef is some distance offshore, requiring a long journey that is usually undertaken in a scary glass-bottomed boat. The reef has recently been threatened by effluent from the chemicals and pesticides used by Queensland's agriculturalists and by something called the Crown of Thorns jellyfish, an evil parasite that is most likely from Overseas. The reef remains one of Australia's greatest assets. One visit, however, could well prove enough.

Germaine Greer

Germaine, who hails from my home town, Melbourne, is a bosom buddy of my erstwhile manager Barry Humphries and a well-known Australian know-all. I have so far not been invited to her rainforest, and I'm not sure I would accept after hearing about all those creepy-crawlies.

She is a world-class champion of women's liberation – an idea she got from me. I well remember Mr and Mrs Greer dropping her off at my Moonee Ponds home when I ran my little drama academy, DEAD (Dame Edna's Academy of Drama). She frequently spun out of control, upsetting the other students, and would probably have been given Ritalin if only it had been invented. I found her a willing learner, and her parents had probably been out of their intellectual depth with her. Of all my students – including Cate Blanchett, Toni Collette, Mel Gibson, little Russell Crowe and even littler Kylie Minogue – she was my favourite, certainly the brightest. She has quite rightly thanked me publicly for the nurturing I gave her, and a little Rome-based Argie friend has tipped me off that she is in line for a rather special honour if – *but only if* – she plays her cards right.

Gum Tree

Where would Australia's cuddly, if vicious, koala (q.v.) be without this popular plant? Australia's world-class bush fires would not have acquired their status without these highly combustible eucalypts. Over the years, gum trees have been welcomed with open arms in many Overseas venues, such as California, Portugal and Madagascar, under the misguided impression that these growing fire bombs would counter soil erosion. This was before it was discovered that a gum tree soaks up forty gallons of water a day, so they are totally unsuitable for protecting lemurs, for example.

A famous ditty of mine contains the couplet 'The best dentists come / From the land of the gum.'

'Australia's world-class bush fires would not have acquired their status without these highly combustible eucalypts'

Hats

In my day the menfolk of Australia, and their womenfolk as well, always wore hats – if they were still in the land of the living! They referred to a special event, such as a garden party at Government House, as a 'hats and glads occasion' ('glads' being the diminutive for Australia's national flower). Nowadays, despite pouring rain and blazing sun, people go bare-headed, protected from the elements by nothing more than a few tattoos and a shaven skull, making for a very spooky look which I hope will just be a passing phase.

We invented the terry-towelling hat, which is still worn at cricket matches and bowls tournaments by senior citizens, and can very easily be tossed into the washing machine when it gets a bit on the grubby side.

The gorgeous Akubra hat is very rarely worn, except by my manager and *éminence grise* Barry Humphries (q.v), who is, to put it mildly, a bit of a poser. 'Akubra' is Aboriginal for rabbit, and the felt for these hats was made from condensed bunnies, which were, in those days, terrible pests, so no one felt all that bad about turning them into millinery. In case you were wondering, there have been no reported cases of myxomatosis

'The hat with corks around the brim was, in fact, a pretty snide British invention'

caused by wearing this headwear, not even in the case of Mr Humphries.

The hat with corks around the brim was, in fact, a pretty snide British invention, and I have never, ever, in all my years in Australia, seen a man thus attired. And since most wine bottles now have screw tops, I think this unsavoury headgear will die a natural death.

The slouch hat, however, which became famous during two world wars, features in the family photo album in many snaps of my uncles and great-uncles. It is, to all intents and purposes, an Akubra with the side turned up and is the subject of a lovely, touching song by Australian vaudevillian and film star George Wallce, which my paternal grandfather used to belt out after a beer or two:

A Brown Slouch Hat

There is a symbol, we love and adore it,
You see it daily wherever you go.
Long years have passed since our fathers once wore it,

What is the symbol that we should all know?

It's a brown slouch hat with the side turned up, and it
    means the world to me.
It is the symbol of our Nation, the land of liberty.
And as soldiers they wear it, how broadly they bear it,
    for all the world to see.
Just a brown slouch hat with the side turned up, heading
    straight for victory.

Don't you thrill as young Bill passes by?
Don't you beam at the gleam in his eye?
Head erect, shoulders square, tunic spick and span,
Ev'ry inch a solider and ev'ry inch a man.

As they swing down the street, aren't they grand?
Three abreast to the beat of the band,
But what do we remember when the boys have passed
    along?
Marching by so brave and strong.

Just a brown slouch hat, etc. . . .

Hills Hoist

This is a rotary metal clothes line which is now a feature of virtually every Australian backyard. It came into being in 1945 in the modest city of Adelaide, where it was invented by Mr Lance Hill, whose wife was sick and tired of running up and down the clothes line. The Hills Hoist took up much less room in suburban backyards than the traditional clothes line with its wooden gallows at each end. Readers should be warned that the hoist can sometimes be a hazard at night-time, when menfolk stumble in the dark between the incinerator and the back door and become, not infrequently, concussed and/or trepanned by the revolving metal rods. On a historical note, when Cyclone Tracy (q.v.) trashed our northern Cinderella city, Darwin, at Christmas 1974, a family claimed that the only thing left standing was the Hills Hoist. What a Christmas!

Recreational Uses: The Hills Hoist is also commonly used in Australian drinking culture in a popular game, Goon of Fortune, involving the hoist and cardboard casks (q.v.) of wine. Quite a few menfolk from the wrong side of the tracks (see under 'Bogans') have fun with their hoists while playing this game. There are many variations of this stimulating pastime but, basically, a cardboard cask of wine (or goon) – another

Australian invention – is strapped to the metal crossbeams of the hoist and the men stand in a circle. They whiz the HH around, and when it stops the closest contestant takes a ten-second glug of the invigorating beverage – red, white or even rosé. The Goon of Fortune has yet to be accepted by the International Olympic Committee as a legitimate event since it is thought that Australians would have an unfair advantage over less thirsty and more abstemious nations.

> PS: I wouldn't be surprised if Mrs Hill gained a considerable amount of weight after her hubbie's invention. By the way, my researchers have found no information whatsoever as to whether there was ever a Mr or Mrs Hoist.

'The Hills Hoist is also commonly used in a popular drinking game, Goon of Fortune'

Hoons

In isolation, hoons are known by their parents to be high-spirited and harmless. They are, in fact, extremely noisy bogans (q.v.). They only function in packs and drive fast cars through sedate neighbourhoods like Moonee Ponds, yelling out of the windows and hurling empty stubbies at respectable citizens going about their business. There is usually an intoxicated girl in their company who will, all too soon, sustain a tummy upset. As a matter of fact, hoons are a universal menace, and it took my ground-breaking homeland to give them a name.

'Hoons are a universal menace, and it took my ground-breaking homeland to give them a name'

Humidicrib

The humidicrib was invented by Edward Thomas Both, an Australian who was responsible for many other medical devices and became known as 'The Edison of Australia'. It is a godsend to premature bubbas as it simulates the mother's tummy. If only my first-born, Lois, had been tucked up in a humidicrib, she may never have been abducted by a feral koala. With a little imagination, humidicribs have many post-natal uses: for example, when an infant has outgrown the facility – and it has been thoroughly cleaned and valeted – it can be used for culinary purposes in the kitchen, such as steaming vegetables, slowly cooking a chook or making a scrumptious steamed pudding.

While on the subject of bubbas, the first frozen embryo was defrosted in my marvellous hometown of Melbourne. How the poor mite was frozen in the first place is beyond the scope of this work. But what a tribute to Melbourne that she chose to thaw there!

Barry Humphries

This person is a failed actor and my long-term manager and, like most managers, has his hands in the till – BIG TIME. It has been rumoured that he and Yours Truly are *the same person*. To which I say: 'What type of home do these people come from, possums?!'

His head can hardly fit inside his Akubra fedora since the inception of the Barry Award, a prize presented to the most outstanding comedy act at the annual Melbourne International Comedy Festival. I don't know about you, possums, but I've always regarded a 'sense of humour' as a rather overrated quality in a person. (This accolade should in no way be confused with the Barry Award, which is a prize awarded annually since 1997 by the editors of *Deadly Pleasures*, an American quarterly publication for crime-fiction readers!)

'I've always regarded a "sense of humour" as a rather overrated quality in a person'

Kangaroo

This is probably the best-known Australian product on the planet and, next to the koala, the one that visitors most wish to cuddle. I have always been very popular with the indigenous community, and they once donated an elderly roo to my furrier so he could make me a cosy winter coat. Other roo lovers have been less fortunate, as the kangaroo, when provoked, enjoys nothing more than eviscerating its admirer, and many Overseas visitors have suffered an inconvenient disembowelment, while others have been stunned by the marsupial's powerful tail.

My Melbourne suburb, Moonee Ponds, has never been a kangaroo hopping ground, and the first one I ever saw was in London Zoo. The poor thing stared at me ruefully through the bars of its eco-friendly prison begging me to repatriate it. I wish I could have swung this, but, as luck would have it, and in spite of my connections, I couldn't spring that particular marsupial. Later, the famous Australian television series *Skippy the Bush Kangaroo* created well-deserved international interest in this adorable animal, and the kangaroo's ability to solve crimes and rescue children in peril was recognised by Save the Children.

STOP PRESS: Scientists from Wollongong and Zurich have pooh-poohed the long-held theory that our main marsupial

'The kangaroo, when provoked, enjoys nothing more than eviscerating its admirer'

omits less greenhouse methane than other creatures, such as smelly New Zealand sheep and cattle. A recent experiment saw red and western grey roos placed in comfortable, sealed chambers with all mod cons, so that their intake and their output of gases could be measured. It came to the conclusion that it's the high-speed way food whizzes through a kangaroo's stomach and not because of inbuilt gut fauna. The scientists are now intent on testing other species for comparison – so hang onto your hats, possums!

If I may wade into the debate: I wouldn't be surprised if all that hopping about has something to do with the phenomenon. There was even a suggestion that kangaroo gut micro-organisms should be transplanted into smelly cows and sheep to decrease their methane output, but I wouldn't fancy a hefty heifer hopping around the place – nor a large merino sheep, for that matter. I personally am not surprised by any of this: after all, fragrance, not flatulence, is an Australian watchword! And I think that goes for the whole nation, except for that embarrassment, Sir Les Patterson!

NB: My late bridesmaid Madge was from New Zealand.

Kangaroo Cranes
(jumping cranes)

No world-class modern-day city worth its salt is complete without a towering forest of kangaroo cranes. To the man in the street it means progress, but to me it means another feather in the multi-plumed hat of Australian inventions, for the kangaroo crane was invented by our own Sir Eric Favelle in the early 1960s. Menfolk of a scientific bent, and certain others, will be interested to learn that it is self-erecting.

The design allows the crane to increase its own height as construction proceeds upwards, and in recent decades it has been used to build many of the world's tallest structures, such as the World Trade Center in New York, the Petronas Towers in Kuala Lumpur and most of the highest buildings in Dubai, including the Burj Khalifa.

'Menfolk of a scientific bent will be interested to learn it is self-erecting'

Ned Kelly

The famous Australian scallywag and folk hero has become a sort of legend and for some reason is venerated by Roman Catholics. When we were kiddies we'd be taken to the Old Melbourne Gaol to view Ned's armour – a few bits of rusty tin he wore during his final stand-off with the law.

The Kelly story became the subject of the world's first feature film, made in Melbourne in 1906. Hollywood came later and, although it was a silent film, it spoke to many Australians at the time and helped Kelly become a folk hero. Since then, there have been many films about him, including one with Mick Jagger as the 'hero'. The artist Sidney Nolan made famous paintings featuring Ned, most of which are in my private collection, housed in a Swiss bank vault.

Speaking of silent films, Yours Truly was once on a chat show alongside Gloria Swanson, an old-world actress in a snood whom Billy Wilder dug up to play the lead in *Sunset Boulevard*. She got *over*-chatty on the show, not having the slightest idea who I was and failing to get the point of me in general. Finally, I had to interject: 'Oh, Miss Swanson, they told me you were a *silent* star.' That certainly put that old minx in her place, possums!

Kiwi Shoe Polish

Kiwi shoe polish has nothing at all to do with our cousins across the sea and is an Australian invention that has kept the shine on our tootsie-wear for decades. It was invented by the Ramsay family and is universally acknowledged to be the best product of its kind in the world. It is becoming a little rarer today since no one cleans their shoes, and if you gave anyone under the age of forty a brush, a rag and a tin of Kiwi, they wouldn't have the faintest idea of what to do with them.

> NB: While I'm on the subject, New Zealanders have allegedly been called 'cultured Australians'. What rubbish, possums!

'Kiwi shoe polish has nothing at all to do with our cousins across the sea'

Koalas
(not bears)

Koalas are probably the most popular marsupials on the planet. Everyone thinks of them as very cuddly but, speaking as someone who has been very badly mauled, if not maimed, by a koala, I tend to disagree. I know they look very sweet, up there in their gum trees, usually sound asleep and, I am told, abusing substances like mad, non-stop, but they have horrible claws hidden in their little furry hands and do not hesitate to lash out, especially at curious and well-meaning tourists from Overseas. On Kangaroo Island, off South Australia, they have become a serious threat, but the Kangaroovians are reluctant

'They look very sweet, up there in their gum trees, usually sound asleep and, I am told, abusing substances like mad'

to instigate a Koalacaust. My first little girl, Lois, about whom I have very rarely spoken, disappeared early one morning from her crib on our sunny Moonee Ponds verandah and was never seen again. A rogue feral koala that had been terrorising the neighbourhood for some weeks was the prime suspect. But the case remains open. . .

> NB: I wouldn't like you to think for a moment that I've got it in for koalas but, no matter what they tell you, and for the record, koalas are definitely *not* bears. No way, José! I actually share my bed with a comforting koala that was humanely culled. It has a Velcroed tummy and contains my hot-water bottle.

Kookaburra

Contrary to popular conception, the kookaburra – or laughing jackass – was not named after Captain James Cook, the discoverer of Australia, who found it no laughing matter when a spear penetrated his person in 1779.

Choosing a bird to represent our country has been the subject of many international competitions. Brolgas and magpies have been seriously considered, while the kookaburra (q.v.) was ultimately disqualified due to its *nom de plumage* and its irreverent, inappropriate, ill-timed outbursts of laughter. Its reptilian diet also went against it being chosen as an image for a tasteful Australian coat of arms. What Overseas person would respect a nation represented by a stocky bird with a snake dangling from its beak?! In the end, the lucky bird elected to embellish the coat of arms was the emu (q.v.).

'Given to irreverent, inappropriate, ill-timed outbursts of laughter'

Lamington

A lamington is a recycled cube of stale, aged sponge cake immersed briefly in molten chocolate and rolled in desiccated coconut. Sydneysiders have been known to add a thin layer of strawberry jam in the middle and, in the 1950s, Australian pâtissiers developed the pink lamington as a popular variation of the scrumptious cake – one that is snapped up during the Gay Pride (q.v.) celebrations in Sydney. The lamington, or 'lammie', is as particular to Australia as the key lime pie is to Key West, the Bakewell tart is to England and the Sachertorte is to Vienna. It was named after Lord Lamington who was Governor of Queensland from 1896 to 1901. There are reports that he did not particularly care for these Australian delicacies, referring to them as 'those bloody, poofy, woolly biscuits'.

> NB: *The Blue Lamington* is a rare and unprocurable – not to say indigestible – 'novel' by my manager Barry Humphries (q.v.). (Not recommended, possums.)

'Those bloody, poofy, woolly biscuits'

Latex Gloves

Latex gloves are gloves made of latex. Whenever my wonderful gyno slaps on his latex gloves before a routine stage-side exploratory before a show, I always think proudly of the anonymous Australian inventor who has saved millions of women from cross-contamination.

'I always think proudly of the anonymous Australian inventor who has saved millions of women from cross-contamination'

Lollies

I was brought up on Violet Crumble bars and it may have affected my natural pigmentation, or at least that of my follicles. This famous confectionery was invented by a Mr Abel Hoadley in the 1930s and consists of a small cube of honeycomb in a raiment of milk chocolate. The only violet aspect of this delicious lolly, however, is its purple wrapper. Over the years I've noticed that Violet Crumble has shrunk a little in size, so that today I'm obliged to eat two – or even more when peckish.

On the subject of lollies – as we Australians call confectionery – I must also mention the Jaffa, a hard ball of chocolate enclosed in a startlingly bright orange, citrus-flavour covering. Traditionally, these are devoured by theatre audiences and are frequently dropped down the steep wooden stairs in the Upper Circle, where their loud descent invariably interrupts the quiet bits of flesh-and-blood shows. This disturbs everyone in my attentive audiences, not just the paupers who release these cascades of lollies from above. They are – and I say this without fear of successful contradiction – Australia's loudest lollies.

Though not exactly a lolly, Arnott's Iced VoVo is a palatable cake invented in Sydney that is regarded in Melbourne as being a bit on the common side. Today's lolly of choice seems to be the Tim Tam (far superior to New Zealand's Chit Chat) which consists of two layers of chocolate malted biscuit encasing a chocolate cream filling and coated with textured chocolate. Inventive as ever, we Australians have come up with a game called the Tim Tam Slam or Tim Tam Suck. Both ends of the Tim Tam are bitten off and one end is dipped into a hot beverage which is sucked through the biscuit as though a straw. It sounds a bit messy to me possums but perhaps I'll try it at Christmas with a nice mulled Australian Shiraz.

'I was brought up on Violet Crumble bars and it may have affected my natural pigmentation'

St Mary MacKillop

Australia got its first saint recently, in the shape of St Mary MacKillop. I'm not sure what miracles she performed, but I'm sure that when the Pope heard how desperate we were in Australia, champing at the bit for our own saint, he probably bent the rules and moved a few goalposts, so that little Mary slipped through without necessarily curing a leper or turning cheap wine into expensive mineral water.

I am often embarrassed by people calling me a saint just because I've changed their lives and actually cured them of something when they attended my wonderful theatre shows. Afterwards, the cleaners have found some pretty spooky things under the seats – teeth, contact lenses, the occasional prosthetic device and even the odd caliper, which does prove that audience members have arrived with something and left without it. I am not taking total credit for this and, up to now, when I gaze in the mirror in the morning I've never noticed much of a glow around my head. It is not just my natural God-given modesty and humility that prevent me from accepting personal sainthood but – and here I do not wish to enter into a sectarian squabble – I am orthodox Church of England (C. of E.). I'm sorry, but I am, and we don't go in for all that stuff,

114

'I am often embarrassed by people calling me a saint just because I've changed their lives and actually cured them of something'

leaving it to the more Irish element of Australian society. Ned Kelly (q.v.), that scallywag of yesteryear, has been practically canonized by generations of Irish Australians, who take him as their role model. Our late prime minister, Mr Gough Whitlam, was a bit of a saint in some people's books for dishing out huge sums of money to Aboriginal lesbian puppeteers and dramaturges. And it has come to my ears that even Germaine Greer has been in the pipeline for a sainthood (on and off), whether she likes it or not. It's funny there are no New Zealand saints since I think you'd have to be a bit of a saint to live there, with all that volcanic activity and the health hazards that go with compulsive nose-rubbing!

I have seen pictures of saints in old churches and, quite frankly, I wouldn't much like to look like them. That is why I hate being called an icon, even though I am. Because women depicted on icons invariably have cracked, yellow faces, with eyes like prunes and rather droopy shoulders and bodies in general. But I think, in my position, I have to keep a pretty open mind. So if you call me a saint, that's your business.

Mallee Root
(a hot Australian root)

A mallee root is a wonderful fuel, once attached to the end of a tree and usually deracinated from a region of Victoria known as the Mallee. These gnarled, nodular old roots glowed in the family grate throughout my childhood, but they are now virtually obsolete and their habitat is a dust bowl. An old friend of our family, who we later heard whispered was of the Unmarried Community and who was known as 'Uncle Max', lived in London during the Second World War and even met Patrick White (q.v.) once in a Turkish bath. Uncle Max told us that he had been in an underground cocktail bar one evening during the Blitz when a big German bomb exploded outside. Asked later about the extent of the blast and its consequences, he quoted a ballet dancer (Robert Helpmann?) who said: 'It blew a chip right off me mallee root pendant, dear.'

> NB: To be described by an Australian as having 'a face like a mallee root' is, under no circumstances, a compliment. It is almost as impolite and uncalled for as that other botanical epithet, 'a face like a half-sucked mango'.

Meat Pie

I quote from a much-loved Australian poem:

Piece in the Form of a Meat Pie

I think that I shall never spy
A poem lovely as a pie.
A banquet in a single course
Blushing with rich tomato sauce.
A pie whose crust is oven kissed,
Whose gravy scalds the eater's wrist.

The pastie and the sausage roll
Have not thy brown mysterious soul.
The dark-hued Aborigine
Is less indigenous than thee.

Like Tom Keneally, rich and chubby,
Tasteful as Patrick White,
With an ice-cold Carlton stubbie
You're the Great Australian Bite.

What Australian schoolchild does not know this mouth-watering verse by somone called J. B. Humphries by heart?

As it happens, the ever-innovative southern metropolis of Adelaide has come up with a somewhat more sophisticated version of the meat pie – the pie-floater or, as they prefer to call it, the *pâté en croûte flottant* – in which the piping-hot pie is literally floated on a dish of thick pea soup until it becomes soup-logged and sinks. Because the hot pie can be volatile, it is recommended that adequate protective clothing be worn at all times – not only by the pie-eater but also by those in his or her immediate proximity. Discriminating gourmets and pie fanciers are advised to obtain this delicacy only from a mobile stall in Victoria Square, next to the Post Office, where they will find it at the peak of its perfection.

'Because the hot pie can be volatile, it is recommended that adequate protective clothing be worn at all times'

Dame Nellie Melba

Whenever we went for a spin in the country outside Melbourne, my wonderful father would drive us through the Yarra Valley and we would marvel at the beautiful gardens, hedges and ferns surrounding Coombe Cottage – the home of our internationally acclaimed warbler, Dame Nellie Melba – where Charlie Chaplin enjoyed a silent dip in her pool (said to be the first swimming pool in Victoria). Inside her mansion, next to some of her microgrooves, there was an old snap of her looking, to my eyes, a bit like a chinless wonder. A lot of things were named after Nellie, including toast and scrummy Peach Melba, which I like smothered with chocolate sauce. I've also heard of Melba gloves, which the diva used to don when she dressed up as a circus ringmaster in a frock coat, complete with a whip and lavender gloves, in order to visit grand English country houses (don't ask, possums).

I myself have had a scrumptious dessert delicacy curated in my honour: Quince Dame Edna.

Melbourne Cup

The Melbourne Cup is the most famous horse race in the world and is run in a suburb of Melbourne called Moonee Valley, a few streets away from my childhood home. 'Moonee' is an old Aboriginal word meaning 'moon' – nothing whatsoever to do with a so-called religious cult or the people who have nothing better to do than put their naked bottoms out of coach windows. The Melbourne Cup is famous for its fashion, in which Australia leads the world. Some years ago, the British glamourpuss Jean Shrimpton ('the Shrimp') caused a hoo-ha when she attended the Cup wearing the first miniskirt seen Down Under. Of course, there has always been a great deal of media interest in what I wear to the event – usually a new creation by my couturier son Kenny, whose gorgeous outfits always get the tongues wagging and which are immediately copied the world over. They can be acquired at his Melbourne boutique Kenny on Collins, my son's salon.

Rupert Murdoch

Many moons ago, in the old home in Moonee Ponds, we had the *Sun News-Pictorial* delivered every day by a little barefoot scamp on a Malvern Star bicycle. When Christmas came around, my father would give generous tips of 2/6d to the dustman and little Rupe, the paper boy. How were we to know that the little turk would stay in the paper business all his life, become a squillionaire and end up at the altar with the Texan glamourpuss Jerry Hall?! What we did not know was that, despite appearances, his parents were very comfortably off and the paper round was just a hobby. When I won the Lovely Mother Competition at the vulnerable age of twenty-one, that little chappie was already a newspaper executive. I suppose he remembered me in my babydoll nightie when I popped out to pick up the papers, and one day he called me into his office with a strange proposal.

'I haven't forgotten that 2/6d your dad used to give me on Christmas Eve, donkey's years ago,' he said, looking over his glasses. When his striking-looking red-haired PA, Becky, had left the room, he continued: 'Now it's payback time, Ms Everage. Page three of my London-based tabloid has always been a boring blank. The Poms need cheering up and I think you're just the girl to fill that space, Edna, so may I view the goods?

'Rest assured, I'm a married man and a Presbyterian.'

'But no one has seen me in my birthday suit, sir,' I said, blushing, 'and my husband Norm has never shown the slightest inclination so to do,' I stuttered. 'What you need is a glamourpuss, and my chests have never been my strong points.'

He touched a bell on his desk and the redheaded minx darted into the room. 'Edna has given me an idea, Becks,' he told her. I was totally confused by that time since I had already slipped out of my underthings, which lay in an incriminating puddle at my feet. The PA shot me a look of disgust. 'Call Damien, our press photographer,' barked Mr M, 'and line up Melbourne's hottest babes. We've nailed page three!'

Blushing and a bit weepy, I gathered up my things and tried to leave the office, with my dignity and top tummies intact. Rupe stopped me. 'Don't worry, Ms Everage,' he said, 'this is the look of tomorrow. One day you and Matilda Swinton will be international turn-ons – pure publishing Viagra!'

And so, for forty-four years, that prediction has come to pass and I've had to brush off menfolk like maggots off a chop at a barbecue. Rupert's vision of me as a sex symbol of the future has come true. I can't speak for Tilda, as she now styles herself...

Neighbours

A long-running and innovative television drama produced by the late Reg Grundy that took the world by storm. It was the first TV series ever to not employ scriptwriters, instead using cleverly concealed cameras to record the everyday lives of typical, sometimes troubled, Australian families. It launched the career of actress and singer Kylie Minogue, one of the earliest graduates of my Dame Edna Academy of Drama (DEAD). As well as Kylie and Germaine Greer, my other alumni include none other than Nicole Kidman, Cate Blanchett, Mel Gibson, Russell Crowe, Hugh Jackman and Olivia Newton-John. I gave Julia Gillard, our one-time prime minister, elocution lessons at the academy after she arrived on our shores with an impenetrably thick Welsh accent. After a few lessons from Yours Truly she acquired a perfectly impenetrable Australian accent.

New Australians

I have read that a surprisingly large percentage of people living in Australia were not born there, and it is getting slightly worse as the whole world begins to realise what Australians knew all along – that it is the greatest little country in the world. Originally, these fugitives from other lands and hostile regimes were known as 'reffos', an affectionate diminutive of 'refugees'. In the 1950s, a more polite term was devised and we began calling them 'New Australians', to give them some motivation.

Many New Australian restaurants cropped up, specialising in spicy or savoury dishes that were not, frankly, to the liking of the average clean-living Australian diner's palate. There had always been Chinese restaurateurs because a lot of Chinamen descended upon us during the gold rush in the mid-nineteenth century to cook scrumptious dishes for the miners in exchange for the odd nugget. It also goes without saying that, in the early days of influxation, ten-pound Poms were two a penny. The term 'New Australian' is now old-fashioned, old-hat and deemed politically incorrect. Most of these newcomers take up Australian nationality so are known as 'paper Aussies'.

Notebook

The notebook, believe it or not, is an Australian invention, and I always travel with a couple so that when I say something particularly clever or witty – a regular occurrence – I can jot it down for posterity. All too often I hear seemingly intelligent people repeating my *aperçus*, zingers and one-liners and getting them slightly wrong, so that's when my notebooks come in handy. With my famed generosity I've bequeathed them to learned institutes, mainly Overseas, even though they may not offer the same tax incentives.

'A hysterectomy in a hospital is not infrequently called a hizzie in a hozzie'

'O' Words
and diminutives

We Australians adore a diminutive – 'dimmies', as we call them. In some cases they are slightly longer than the original words. We had a neighbour called Steve who was always known as 'Stevo'. A hysterectomy in a hospital is not infrequently called a 'hizzie in a hozzie', and the letter 'O' comes into its own in wonderful words such as 'garbos' (garbage collectors), 'reffos' (refugees), 'paedos' (paedophiles), 'journos' (journalists), 'deros' (derelicts), 'smokos' (a break from work for a cigarette or two), 'musos' (musicians), 'alcos' (alcoholics), 'gynos' (gynaecologists), Lebbos (Lebanese) and lezzos (lesbians). It must be borne in mind that Australian speech is designed for ease of utterance and to obviate, as much as possible, the opening of the mouth and the use of vocal cords. This is mainly down to attempting to avoid ingesting flying insects. Anyway, who wants to say 'garbage collector' when 'garbo' will do? As it happens, posher Australians have been known to refer to these operatives as 'garbologists'.

Ocker

Related to the word 'oik' or 'yokel', the ocker is a very common type of Australian male who lets the side down on an international level. My nephew from Sydney, Barry McKenzie, was the original ocker, and he was quickly imitated – in a 'ripped' sort of way – by a Paul Hogan, who also hopped on the ocker bandwagon by pretending to be one, which is a strange practice, since, with the greatest respect, most Australian men are already ockers by nature.

'A very common type of Australian male who lets the side down on an international level'

Pacemaker

Many people throughout the world have taken Australia to their hearts, and I mean that literally, as the pacemaker was invented in 1926 by Dr Mark C. Lidwell at Royal Prince Alfred Hospital, Sydney, and it has saved lives all over the planet. My late husband, Lord Everage of Moonee Ponds, was kept ticking over by a very early version of this miracle machine and, even more, by an expensive device called a prostate governor, or 'Prostmaker', to normalise his unpredictable plumbing, but let's not go there, possums...

'Many people throughout the world have taken Australia to their hearts, and I mean that literally'

Pavlova
(or Pav)

Created in the Esplanade Hotel, Perth, the pavlova is a
swirly meringue concoction with a crisp crust and soft, light
inside set like marshmallow, best served with a generous
slathering of whipped cream and lusciously smothered with
various fruits, such as pineapple, strawberries (strawbs) and
other berries, kiwi fruit and, most essential of all, *passion fruit*.

New Zealand, in a long discredited, typically despicable
claim, attempted to gain credit for the creation of this now
internationally loved queen of desserts – I suppose just
because there is sometimes the odd chunk of kiwi fruit
included (which is actually Chinese gooseberry anyway!). It
was named after Anna Pavlova, the Russian ballerina who
danced her way into Australian hearts with her 1920s tours.

Ironically, today's figure-conscious dancers are contractually
forbidden to ingest this scrumptious, cholesterol-laden,
calorific Australian delicacy.

'I always liked a man with a nice vertical crease'

Permanent Crease

Lord Norm Everage always seemed to have problems with his trousers – or 'strides', as he called them – particularly in his later years. I was frequently on my knees in front of him with a hair dryer, making my husband presentable. I always liked a man with a nice vertical crease; and then along came an Australian invention – permanent-crease clothing, which was a godsend to women of all breeds and classes who were too busy to erect the ironing board and press a loved one's garments to perfection with an old-fashioned iron! The pleated skirt is a fashion item of yesteryear and one that has come back into fashion, and it was in maintaining the corrugation on such skirts that permanent creasing came into its own. My bridesmaid Madge was permanently rumpled and could certainly have done with an injection from the clever scientists at the CSIRO laboratories.

Phar Lap
(Australia's Wonder Horse)

An Australian icon and world-famous thoroughbred gee-gee whose mounted hide is displayed in the Melbourne Museum. His heart ended up at the National Museum of Australia and his skeleton has pride of place in the Museum of New Zealand Te Papa Tongarewa. When we were knee-high to grasshoppers, my father would take us to the world-class museum and art gallery to gaze at this famous steed, though we were never really sure why. Poor old Phar Lap passed away in America, and it was said he was murdered on the orders of American gangsters, nervous that he might spoil their gambling investments.

NB: It was only during my meticulous research for this book that I discovered that the steed's name has nothing to do with a lap of a horse race but is a translation of a Thai word for 'lightning'.

Plastic (Polymer) Bank Notes

Australian paper money was always a problem since most of it spent a good deal of time getting soggy on the bar surfaces of refreshment rooms. We invented waterproof, wipe-clean money in 1988, and it has since been copied worldwide, including in Kuwait, and, more recently, Great Britain.

Before the advent of plastic money, Australian menfolk would often be embarrassed after returning in the small hours to find their wives demanding housekeeping money, only to find it saturated with Foster's lager or some other nice beverage. Imagine how the housewives and homemakers felt when they went shopping later that day and the proffered money reeked of the night before, when their hubbies had been out carousing. As a result, they successfully petitioned the government to come up with something to avoid this social embarrassment.

Plastic Spectacle Lenses

I am, of course, renowned for my specs, but it might come as a surprise to my fans that my eyesight is twenty–twenty, so there are no lenses in my fabulous face furniture. They are just frames for my internationally acclaimed eyes. Nana Mouskouri, Maria Callas, Elton John, Elvis Costello, Su Pollard and Alan Carr will spring to mind (except for the last couple) as copiers of my look. However, if you do need lenses in your glasses – particularly if you are a pauper sitting high up at one of my shows – once again Australia has come to the rescue. For it was in Australia in 1960 that foreseeing Australian scientists in Adelaide invented the first plastic optical lens. These lenses are unbreakable, washable and light as a feather.

'There are no lenses in my fabulous face furniture'

Platypus

The platypus is one of Australia's most endearing inventions. Neither fish nor fowl, it is an eye-boggling marsupial with a duck's bill, webbed feet and a silky waterproof pelt. When a stuffed one was first taken to Britain it was pooh-poohed by zoologists, who supposed that some 'wag' in Australia had stitched a few marsupials and the odd duck together to bamboozle know-all members of the scientific community. Luckily, they are still not extinct since they are inedible and very rarely crop up in Aboriginal cookbooks. Even their eggs are not a breakfast item. They look very cute as they slither along the creek but, like koalas (q.v.), they are vicious creatures, being equipped with poisonous spurs which they do not hesitate to use on some unsuspecting paddler.

Polly Waffle

Yet another Melbourne invention, this popular pan-Australian confectionery was conceived in the 1940s by Mayfield B. Anthony, accountant and friend of the fabled Hoadley family. It consisted of a marshmallow core encrusted with nodular chocolate. The mouth-watering 1970s advertising slogan was 'Mmm, crunch, aaah!' There was universal sadness when, around 23 November 2009, it was announced that the Polly Waffle industry had ground to a halt and would cease operation due to poor sales.

I hate to lower the tone of my book, possums, but for the record, common people, including politicians, used to refer to their 'jobbies' as Polly Waffles. In Parliament a member once described a budget as 'about as popular as a Polly Waffle floating in a public swimming pool'. When my nephew Russell,

'The mouth-watering 1970s advertising slogan was "Mmm, crunch, aaah!"'

who could get a bit on the vulgar side, heard this he added: 'Or as popular as a funnel web spider in a lucky dip'.

NB: I am pleased and relieved to tell readers that the Polly Waffle has recently received a reprieve and has been brought back – as a result of online fury – under a new name: The Great Aussie Waffle Log.

NB: Nephew Russell was the black sheep of the family and a pilot for a while, until he was dismissed for fornication and drunkenness on the flight deck. He had many colourful aeronautical expressions which used to puzzle me. For years he talked about 'dangling the Dunlops', for instance. Turned out it meant to lower the wheels of an aircraft for landing, as in: 'I'll be dangling the Dunlops over Darwin next week'.

Possums

My mother invariably called us 'possums'. By 'us' I mean me and my siblings Laurie and Athol (though I've always thought of myself as an only child with a couple of brothers). I don't know where she got the appellation, but later I adopted it as an affectionate term of endearment. Americans don't regard it as a compliment if you call them possums. Mind you, possums, Americans don't get the point of a lot of things, let's face it. They didn't come to England during the Gulf War because they thought the English Channel was the Gulf, and I'd wager good money if any of them in the White House knew the difference between Iraq and Iran or even where they are. American possums are a bit different from their Australian cousins. Cuddle one and you will soon find out, receiving deep facial scars to prove it.

In the old days of Moonee Ponds, before it became an elite suburb on a par with London's Belgravia, San Francisco's Pacific Heights and the Upper East Side of New York City, we had a corrugated iron roof, long before they became fashionable. At night we could hear those possums clattering around above our heads and sometimes even trying for a family. They were a blessed nuisance, as Australia was at the sharp end of the conservation movement. (By the way, I am a human rights lawyer emeritus, and I'm fighting to get the Elgin Marbles for Melbourne, which has been described as the second largest Greek city on the planet.) When our possums got out of control, we'd call Mr Possoff, a Polish chappie with a van. He would climb onto the roof and whisk them away, saying he would drop them off at the Botanical Gardens. But I found out later that he usually relocated those pesky marsupials to the roof of the people next door, and pretty soon, even at that distance, we could hear them scampering about and resuming their nocturnal attempts at a family. But let's face it, fans, when you're at one of my shows I tend to think that you'd prefer to be called possums rather than some of the other marsupials inhabiting our wide brown land, which, to name just a few, include quolls, dibblers, mulgaras, ningauis, wambergers, kowaris, numbats, bilbies, pademelons, potoroos, dunnarts or even little red kalutas! 'Hello, dibblers', for example, doesn't have the same ring to it. . .

'Americans don't regard it as a compliment if you call them possums'

Refrigeration

Anyone who enjoys a chilled lager or a table wine at the correct temperature – and include me in this – should raise a glass to salute Australia, the island continent where refrigeration as we know it was invented. This was confirmed as long ago as 1967 by none other than the world-class Australian Institute of Refrigeration, which threw cold water over any other impertinent claimants, saying that the Melbourne printer, James Harrison, was 'unquestionably the authentic practical inventor of commercial refrigeration'.

'Raise a glass to salute Australia, the island continent where refrigeration as we know it was invented'

ResMed

Like many of the menfolk of my acquaintance, my husband, Lord Norm, snored like a trooper. He not only snored, but chatted away like a magpie. A lot of his chat was about his traumatic experiences during the Second World War when thought he was having a bayonet stuck in him by a Jap, which was a bit silly since he'd never been in the War.

In those days we didn't know about 'sleep apnea', a serious condition which took an Australian, Colin Edward Sullivan, with his wonderful invention – a flattering plastic mask manufactured by the ResMed company – worn by the somnolent individual and attached to a computer which promotes a healthy flow of oxygen and even extends the sleeper's life, should he or she wake up.

Royal Flying Doctor Service

Australia is a place in which it is not desirable to fall ill or throw a sickie, since, in the Olden Days, a visit from the doctor could take as long as three months (almost as long as British patients must wait for an appointment with a doctor in their cutting-edge National Health Service). In 1928, all this changed with the advent of the Flying Doctor Service, whose healthcare professionals took to the air and brought wellness to remote sufferers. This has been expanded dramatically and the air is now teeming with flying gynos, chiropodists and dentists. And, as this goes to press, it's 'chocks away' for the world's first flying proctologist.

'The air is now teeming with flying gynos, chiropodists and dentists'

Shark

The shark is not an indigenous Australian, but it is known to oceanographers and marine biologists as a fish with a distinct preference for Australian waters and the world-class Australian swimmers therein. Circling the continent in their endless quest for human company, the creatures are completely harmless, unless they bite you. Fortunately, up to now they have never been known to present a danger in continental Australia, unlike the dingo or funnel-web spider. Sharks starred in several films in the 1970s and '80s and were known everywhere, except in Australia, as 'Noahs'. Their succulent white meat is sensitively marketed as 'flake', which is a principal constituent of fish and chips *à l'australienne*.

STOP PRESS: Fisheries Research Director Rick Fletcher recently said that there have been reports of shark breeding grounds in the Great Australian Bight! But I don't think that's how the great inlet got its name.

Southern Cross

The Southern Cross, the spectacular constellation that hangs above my homeland, is not an Australian invention, but Dame Nature certainly wouldn't bat an eyelid if we Australians appropriated it. It shines on us all through our unpolluted skies and inspired the inclusion of the five stars which appear on our flag, along with a seven-pointed-star (the Commonwealth Star) representing the Australian states and territories, making a total of six stars altogether. Sadly, New Zealand's flag only runs to four stars – it is really spooky how the Man Upstairs has rated our two nations.

> NB: There was a move by the jealous Kiwis to drop the star system altogether and to replace it with a design that resembled a beach towel. However, this was defeated in a referendum, so New Zealand remains a four star nation.

'Sadly, New Zealand's flag only runs to four stars'

'Snugly fitting swimwear for immodest menfolk'

Speedos

Speedos are snugly fitting swimwear for immodest menfolk. My late husband, Lord Norm, in his swimming days, when he was not attached to his prostate governor, always wore a pair of fawn or maroon Jantzens – a woollen costume consisting of shorts with a woollen panel at the front to conceal any offensive contours that might arise. They were known as 'togs' in Melbourne and, in Sydney, 'cozzies', and they always had a canvas belt with a rusty buckle. Speedos were invented in 1914 by Alexander MacRae and were popularised by foreign show-offs and unmarried men who would recline on the beach as though posing for an uncalled-for painting by Lucian Freud. When I was going through my son Kenny's room once I found a magazine that looked like a swimwear catalogue, but on further inspection it turned out to be something else, so I quickly put it back in the drawer. Today's male cozzies and togs are often referred to as 'budgie smugglers' but how our 'native' bird could survive cooped up in there is beyond the scope of this publication.

Spray-on Skin

An invention from stiflingly hot Western Australia (c.1993) used for the treatment of burns and serious epidermal damage. In certain remote areas it is known to have been used in large quantities for racial reassignment. My Kiwi bridesmaid, the late Mrs Madge Allsop, was a pioneer when the treatment was at its teething stage, seizing upon the invention and recklessly having her whole body anointed, but to no avail: the contraction of her tegument increased her resemblance to the bog woman of Koelbjerg. I personally think that spending her childhood acting the goat around boiling New Zealand geysers was the cause of her pitiful condition.

Joan Sutherland

Dame Joan Sutherland was Australia's greatest soprano and, like many other dames, a close personal buddy of mine. Although an international diva, 'La Stupenda' was always natural and unaffected, and when I used to visit her in her Swiss chalet her greatest pleasure was to hear me sing ditties from the Great Australian Song Book. Sadly, Joan is no longer with us, but I can still imagine her trilling snippets from Michael Tippett's rarely revived opera *The Knot Garden*. Who else in the musical world could trill Tippett snippets from that challenging work, I ask you?

'Australia's greatest soprano and, like many other dames, a close personal buddy of mine'

Swagman
(or swaggie)

During my wonderful childhood, if we ever went for a spin to the country on a Sunday afternoon, I would ask my father to take us to see some swaggies. We'd occasionally spot them under a river gum beside Moonee Ponds Creek, and they normally wore old khaki army greatcoats, since the majority of swaggies were ex-servicemen who had not been successfully reintroduced into polite society. Today they'd probably be attempting to the sell *The Big Issue*. If we were very lucky, we might even have caught sight of an old swaggie with an actual swag, attempting to boil a billy and singing 'Waltzing Matilda', a lovely ditty that you should look up on YouTube, possums.

I have to say that the swaggies we glimpsed from our speedy Oldsmobile were very rarely jolly or stuffing jumbucks.

NB: 'Waltzing Matilda' with Banjo Paterson's 1895 lyric, published with sheet music in 1903, is the unofficial national anthem of Australia. Waltzing Matilda Day (6 April) marks the anniversary of the first performance of this classic at a homestead near Winton in Queensland.

Once a jolly swagman camped by a billabong
Under the shade of a coolibah tree,
And he sang as he watched and waited till his billy boiled:
'Who'll come a-waltzing Matilda, with me?'

Waltzing Matilda, waltzing Matilda
You'll come a-waltzing Matilda, with me
And he sang as he watched and waited till his billy boiled:
'You'll come a-waltzing Matilda, with me.'

Down came a jumbuck to drink at that billabong.
Up jumped the swagman and grabbed him with glee.
And he sang as he shoved that jumbuck in his tucker bag:
'You'll come a-waltzing Matilda, with me.'

(Chorus)

Up rode the squatter, mounted on his thoroughbred.
Down came the troopers, one, two, and three.
'Whose is that jumbuck you've got in your tucker bag?
You'll come a-waltzing Matilda, with me.'

(Chorus)

Up jumped the swagman and sprang into the billabong.
'You'll never take me alive!' said he
And his ghost may be heard as you pass by that billabong:
'Who'll come a-waltzing Matilda, with me?'

(Chorus)

Sydney Funnel-web Spider
(atrax robustus)

Australia's most iconic and popular arachnid creepy-crawly. This furry fellow lurks in Sydney's northern suburbs. When it isn't basking lazily by the swimming pool its favourite haven is the warm and humid environment of the bedside slipper. One of my favourite James Bond films, *Dr No*, shows Sir Sean Connery in bed without his jimjams, watching a webbo (as it is affectionately called) creep over his shoulder. I asked my dear friend Sean whether it was very scary, but he said, 'They used a stunt man.' 'But how', I asked, not unreasonably, 'could the stunt man fit into the spider costume?' He just gave me one of his famous funny looks.

Atrax robustus is one of three species of the genus *Atrax*, another being *Atrax sutherlandi*, which, I am assured, has nothing to do with Joan (q.v.), who was another of my dearest intimates.

Sydney Gay Pride

My experience in the upper echelons of show business has taught me a few spooky facts about human nature, and perhaps the hardest one to swallow is that there are fellow humans – yes, women as well as men – who, when it comes to the crunch, prefer to cuddle members of their own gender. I yield to no one in my abhorrence of homophobia and I am aware that these words are being read by my hairdressers, travel agents, choreographers, florists, favourite air stewards and stage designers, but I believe that these folk are all passing – if rather slowly – through a *phase*. For ages this proclivity was thought by many to be an Australian invention, and I'm relieved and happy to say it isn't. Since then, uncalled-for frescoes in Pompeii have been uncovered indicating that the ancient Romans passed through similar phases themselves. Happily, our Aboriginal rock frescoes do not depict such acts of immodesty!

Sydney has a famous procession in which troubled young people from broken homes – often attired in the *habillements* of the opposite sex – cavort on floats and on the back of 'utes' (q.v.), letting off steam. Not to put too fine a point on it, *grown men dressed as women* – yuk!

At one point the Authorities in South Australia made it compulsory to be so-called 'gay'. And, incidentally, I've met very few people of this persuasion who seem all that happy about it. Of course, famous people like me, with their heads above the parapet, attract evil gossip, and the rumours about my couturiers (etc., as above) having such proclivities is sheer paper talk. Strangely enough, my San Francisco-based son Kenny and his chum Clifford Smail are usually in Sydney around the time that all this nonsense takes place.

Even more of a coincidence: my daughter Valmai and her girl chums, Ellen, Fran, Trish, Bobby, Shapelle, Tommy, Kay, Martina, Radclyffe and Jeanette, for some reason all turn up for the same event – quite a few of them on motorbikes.

'Not to put too fine a point on it, grown men dressed as women – yuk!'

Sydney Harbour Bridge
(the coathanger)

This Sydney-based construction is one of Australia's most over-rated icons. Frankly, possums, it's not a patch on Melbourne's Princes Bridge, which is toll-free and does not need to be painted all year round, which explains why most of Sydney's motor vehicles are splattered with deadly lead paint. The only point in crossing the Sydney Harbour Bridge is if you want to go to North Sydney, home of the deadly funnel-web spider (q.v.), so not a destination I would recommend. It took many years to construct after the first sod was turned in 1923, and although the bridge was opened in 1932, they've apparently never managed to pay it off – or so it is said by my colleagues in Melbourne.

'One of Australia's most over-rated icons'

Sydney Opera House

In the early 1950s, when I was a kiddie but already tipped as an embryonic megastar, the world-class conurbation of Sydney had a big problem: what to put on the postage stamps. Her Majesty the Queen, naturally, but first of all the Authorities ran through all the marsupials as possibilities. The platypus was a dead duck and Aboriginal warriors had begun to pall. 'What about a historic building?' suggested a political veteran. 'I thought all those old-fashioned bastards had been pulled down,' interjected another elder statesman. From the cut and thrust of this debate emerged a plan to create a brand-new building, and almost every politician in New South Wales, along with their wives, families, significant others and same-sex partners, went on long fact-finding missions around the world, at the taxpayers' expense, to see what could grace our stamps. The final consensus, agonizingly reached, was to build an opera house, examples of which some of our fact-finders had glimpsed in foreign cities during their shopping expeditions. Of course, they all agreed that the proposed erection need not necessarily stage operas as such, but could be a convention centre, child-minding facility, supermarket or – and here they employed a new word never before articulated in Australia – a *venue* (pronounced 'vee-new'). A competition was launched across the globe, and the controversial winner was a Dane from Denmark, Jørn Utzon. His inspiration came to him in the middle of one of his smorgasbords, when he spotted a napkin folded in a fancy Danish way that suggested mountain peaks or the sails of a ship. His scribbled design won favour in Sydney, as well as a good deal of ridicule, with Australian-based architects protesting against the Scandinavian interloper.

The building that now stands on Bennelong Point can still present small operas, in spite of local politicos insisting on banishing the planned opera auditorium to a smaller hall, leaving the larger one for *proper* shows. A visiting UK-based composer, Benjamin Britten, was shown over the opera house in its formative stages and was proudly shown the orchestra pit of the opera auditorium. 'We can fit a whole orchestra in there, Sir Benjamin,' proclaimed Senator Brendan Doig, the minister for culture, proudly. 'I suppose if they're all Japanese playing piccolos,' riposted the snide, unmarried, English smart aleck.

Thong

The thong is a simple rubber or plastic item of footwear known elsewhere as a flip-flop and in New Zealand as a jandal. Thongs were the universal casual footwear of choice for discriminating people and, until the advent of the Croc, uniquely suited for the outdoor activities enjoyed by most Australians. There are some conservative institutions that discriminate against thonged people, even when they are attired in suits and ties or full-length ballgowns, and most of the more upscale bars and restaurants still have a sign outside their doors bearing the legend 'Sorry, no thongs'. In Darwin, northern Australia, however, thongs are *de rigueur* with formal attire, and it is not unusual to see a placard outside a place of entertainment saying, 'Thongs and singlets must be worn at all times.'

'Thongs were the universal casual footwear of choice for discriminating people, until the advent of the Croc'

The Three
Sisters

Australia's Mount Rushmore, this geological formation, in the Blue Mountains just outside Sydney, is so called because of its uncanny resemblance to three famous Australian women: Germaine Greer, Pauline Hanson and little Nicole Kidman (even though the last was born in Honolulu). The Aboriginal names of these outcrops are Meehni (922 metres), Wimlah (918 metres) and Gunnedoo (906 metres), but I don't think these would look very good on a book, political pamphlet or movie poster. Frankly, looking at these craggy lumps, I am grateful none of them has ever been thought to look in the least like Yours Truly.

The Twelve Apostles

Located on the shores of the Southern Ocean, across
from Tasmania in Australia's Marine National Park, these
internationally acclaimed monoliths give a pretty good idea
of what the original apostles must have looked like in real
life, even though there were just nine rock stacks when the
formation received its name (don't ask, possums). One of the
apostles collapsed dramatically in July 2005 – and then there
were eight.

*'There were just nine rock stacks
when the formation received its
name (don't ask, possums)'*

Ugg Boots

The name says it all, possums. These snug environments for the feet have swept the world and are occasionally worn inappropriately by women in evening dress or even bridesmaid's attire. Though admittedly very practical, they have now made their way onto the haute couture catwalk. The iconic Ugg boot is made of soft twin-face sheepskin, with the fleece on the inside, and a synthetic sole. They are the footwear of choice for bogans (q.v.) and those with a 'daggy' fashion sense, including the surfing community.

'The name says it all, possums'

Uluru

A world-class natural rock installation in the middle of Australia which records show has been in place at least since early 1887. A dome-shaped red rock, it has been in the same location ever since. It is our Stonehenge but, paradoxically enough, no Druid has ever been known to set foot on it! The reasons for its construction have been lost in the mists of Dreamtime and no one knows what Uluru means in modern-day Australian, though ignorant and misleading tourist guides pretend they do. My theory is that it means 'very large red rock'. For shameful decades it was known as Ayers Rock (who he, possums?), but happily it has reverted to its original name. There was national fury when a property developer, affiliated with the hospitality industry, suggested Uluru be hollowed out and turned into a world-class, very large, boutique hotel, spa, indoor climbing facility and conference centre. I'm pleased and relieved to inform you that – even though some money changed hands – this appalling suggestion never got past the drawing-board stage.

Ute

The word 'ute' is an abridgement of an Australian invention: the utility truck, a monocoque vehicle particularly popular with rural folk that is known in the US as a pick-up. Quite frankly, I've never been a driver or passenger, front or back, in one of these vehicles. I am told that young couples like to have a 'lie down' in the back bit. And if they're not doing that, they use it for the storage of animals, infants and shopping, and, on special occasions, for transporting outsize wedding presents.

'Quite frankly, I've never been a driver or passenger, front or back, in one of these vehicles'

Vegemite

An edible brown ointment, Vegemite is believed to be the residue of the ale-making process and is a popular spread for toast at most Australian breakfasts. Many world-class Australian athletes, singers and celebrities in general were brought up on it from the cradle. Its rival, Marmite, is often said to be an acquired taste – i.e. you love it or hate it – but with Vegemite there is no such equivocation and, for the connoisseur, no such quandary. Vegemite has been immortalised in song by my late friend and fellow chanteuse, Eartha Kitt: 'I want to wake up in the morning with that dark brown taste...'

No vegetables are harmed in the making of Vegemite and it is therefore safe for vegetarians as a flavouring for stews, gravies, etc. In 2011 there was an international incident when President Obama said Vegemite tasted 'horrible'!

'Its rival, Marmite, is often said to be an acquired taste but with Vegemite there is no such equivocation'

Wattle
(acacia pycnantha)

This gorgeous bloom is Australian mimosa; or perhaps it is French wattle. In marvellous Melbourne, where I spent my historic formative years, the wattle used to bloom in all its glory in June. Not far from our home in Humoresque Street, Moonee Ponds (now a heritage site and place of pilgrimage – a bit like that zebra crossing in St John's Wood, London, which is usually swarming with Oriental photographers who have never heard of the Beatles), there lived a little French family who had a way with wattle. French people were few and far between in Australia, and we always thought they only came to our internationally acclaimed country if they had done something wrong in France and blotted their copybooks. This was usually the case. The LaSalles – Pierre and his wife – used to harvest the wattle and gobble up the little yellow fluffy balls, solidified in a sugary syrup. I believe that in Grasse, France, they call this *praline mimosa*. I once overheard a neighbour of ours make a rude remark: 'Those bloody frogs will eat anything.' It was a remark that was uncalled for but had also an inescapable ring of truth.

Patrick White

A severe, censorious, Nobel Prize-winning Australian novelist and playwright whose books I have been trying to read for yonks. He has unkindly been described as an Australian Lady Bracknell. Literary friends tell me that he modelled some of his characters on me, and they don't, apparently, bring out my nice side. I always thought he was a bit of an old curmudgeon, but he was a pussycat at heart and we often went on long marches together – Save the Bandicoot, for example, and Anti-Discrimination Against Aboriginal Lesbianism in Women's Prisons.

'Literary friends tell me that he modelled some of his characters on me, and they don't, apparently, bring out my nice side'

Wine Casks
(aka goons)

The wine cask is a world-renowned Australian invention consisting of a cardboard box with a plastic handle containing a bladder of wine that can be poured via a plastic spigot on the side. They are extremely popular with domestic sippers and alcoholic housewives, who keep them in the fridge and avail themselves of their contents throughout the day when their husbands are at work. The main advantage of the cask is that the family will never see the level of wine drop, though there may be other evidence of diurnal consumption when the hungry family returns home to find mother sleeping peacefully on the kitchen floor, out for the count, with the fridge door ajar.

'The main advantage of the cask is that the family will never see the level of wine drop'

Woop Woop

A place in Western Australia with nothing to appeal to anyone, not even the most curious tourist, which has led to expressions such as 'He lives out in (the) woop woop.' Other expressive Australian terms for the back of beyond are 'beyond the black stump' and the 'Never Never'. 'Woop woop' is said to have been derived from the nickname given to men who carried fleeces in shearing sheds, taken from the sound they made as they ran around. Sounds rather far-fetched to me, possums!

Wowsers

A wowser is an Australian killjoy or puritan, and it is hardly necessary to tell you that the epithet has never been flung at me. I regret to say that my Kiwi bridesmaid, the late Mrs Madge Allsop, was a bit of a wowser: she was always jealous of me having fun and, as a result, turned her nose up at anything amusing or slightly naughty. She didn't mature until very late in life, when, I'm sorry to say, she went to the other extreme and spun out of control.

> NB: The word 'wowser' is an acronym that comes from a nineteenth-century Australian temperance slogan, 'We Only Want Social Evils Remedied'.

'A wowser is an Australian killjoy or puritan, and it is hardly necessary to tell you that the epithet has never been flung at me'

Zinc Cream

Zinc cream was developed by Faulding Pharmaceutical in 1940 to guard against nappy rash, athlete's foot and poison ivy. For a bit of fun, some people have been known to colour the cream with fluorescent material. When we were knee-high to grasshoppers and playing with buckets and spades on Australia's cutting-edge beaches, our mothers always insisted that we had a great smear of zinc cream on our noses, cheeks and lips to protect us from spooky things called ultra-violet rays. The unguent was snapped up by the cricketing community, who nowadays cover their faces with white stripes that remind me of our wonderful indigenous folk when they corroborate with each other. Today no self-respecting cricketer, tennis player or surfer worth his salt goes about his business unanointed.

'No self-respecting cricketer worth his salt goes about his business unanointed'

Thanks

Edna wishes to thank her little helpers:
Wendy Brown, Sarah Dridan, Marina Foster,
Barry Humphries, Jared Kelly, David Lucas,
Aden McConville, Cat McConville, Lynda
O'Connor, Lyn Schwan, Lizzie Spender, Brian
Thomson and Ken Thomson.

First published in the UK in 2016 by Head of Zeus Ltd

1 3 5 7 9 10 8 6 4 2

A catalogue record for this book is available from the British Library.

ISBN (HB) 9781784975609
(E) 9781784975593

Photography by Larry Rostant
Artworking by Lorna Brown

Printed and bound in China by 1010 Printing International Ltd

Head of Zeus Ltd
Clerkenwell Green
45–47 Clerkenwell Green
London EC1R 0HT

WWW.HEADOFZEUS.COM